This book belongs to:

_____

This book is dedicated to all my precious former students, and to all the loving parents and caregivers out there who are working to ensure their children feel sunny inside.

Also to my loyal family and friends, you fill my heart with glee!

And Mark, thank you for being you.

Dear Parents or Caregivers,

This book is intended to be read to your child from page 37 on or in its entirety.
Please attach a photo of your child on page 46.

Warm Regards,

Glyncora Murphy

Printed in the United States of America
First Printing, 2014
ISBN-13: 978-0-9885510-7-7
ISBN-10: 0988551071
LCCN: 2012921335

For permission requests, write to the publisher, addressed
"Attention: Permissions Coordinator," at the address below.
pc@babyblanketpress.com
Baby Blanket Press
New York, NY
www.babyblanketpress.com

Thanks To A Wonderful Creative Team
Illustrator: Jesse Stern
Editor: Erika Wilder
Post-Production and Book Design: Nakiska Shaikh
Post-Production: Justin Troust of Second Sight Art + Color
Photography and Post-Production: George Evan
Photography: Mark Murphy

BABY
BLANKET
PRESS

I Love You, Favorite Present

A surprise in a story is a wonderful thing...

Do you have a favorite gift?

One that fills you up with love?

A very favorite present

That you're always thinking of ?

Just like finding a rare pearl

In a teeny oyster shell,

You can look at this book's pages

For a present show-and-tell.

Pablo's favorite present is a silver telescope.

He counts the craters in the moon while friends are jumping rope!

When planets shine so brightly
In a navy sky with stars,

He travels to a distant place:

A moon with stunning scars!

"I love you, favorite present;

You fill my heart with glee!

My life got so much better,

The day you came to me."

Twyla's favorite present is a kitty-cat named Wonder.

She holds her kitty closely, when she hears the roar of thunder.

If lightning strikes the pavement,

And the shutters start to shake...

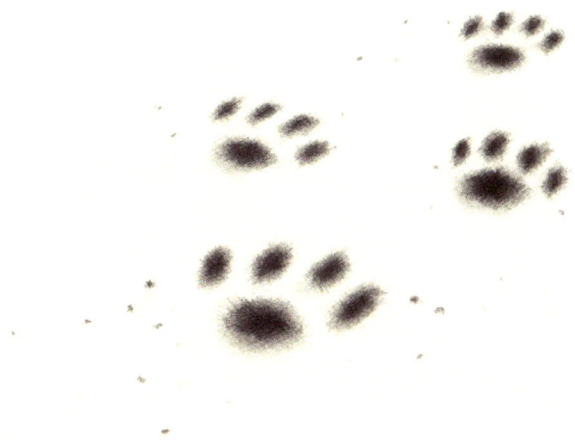

She cuddles with her kitty-cat,

And dreams of birthday cake.

"I love you, favorite present;

You fill my heart with glee!

My life got so much better,

The day you came to me."

Adam's favorite present is a soldier made of wood.

This soldier helps reveal a world of happiness and good.

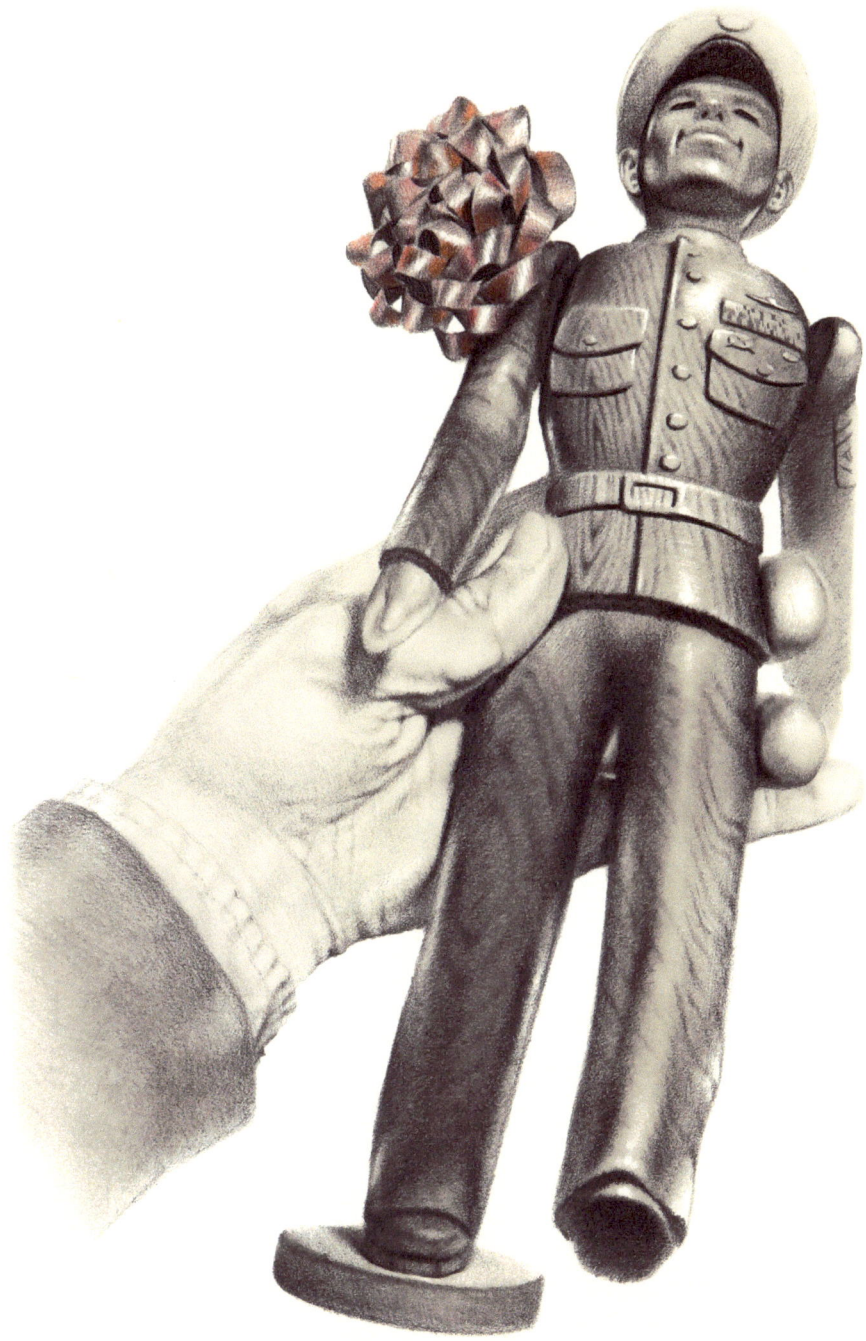

If Adam feels the sadness

When his father needs to go,

He reaches for his wooden toy,

And holds a puppet show.

23

"I love you, favorite present;

You fill my heart with glee!

My life got so much better,

"The day you came to me."

25

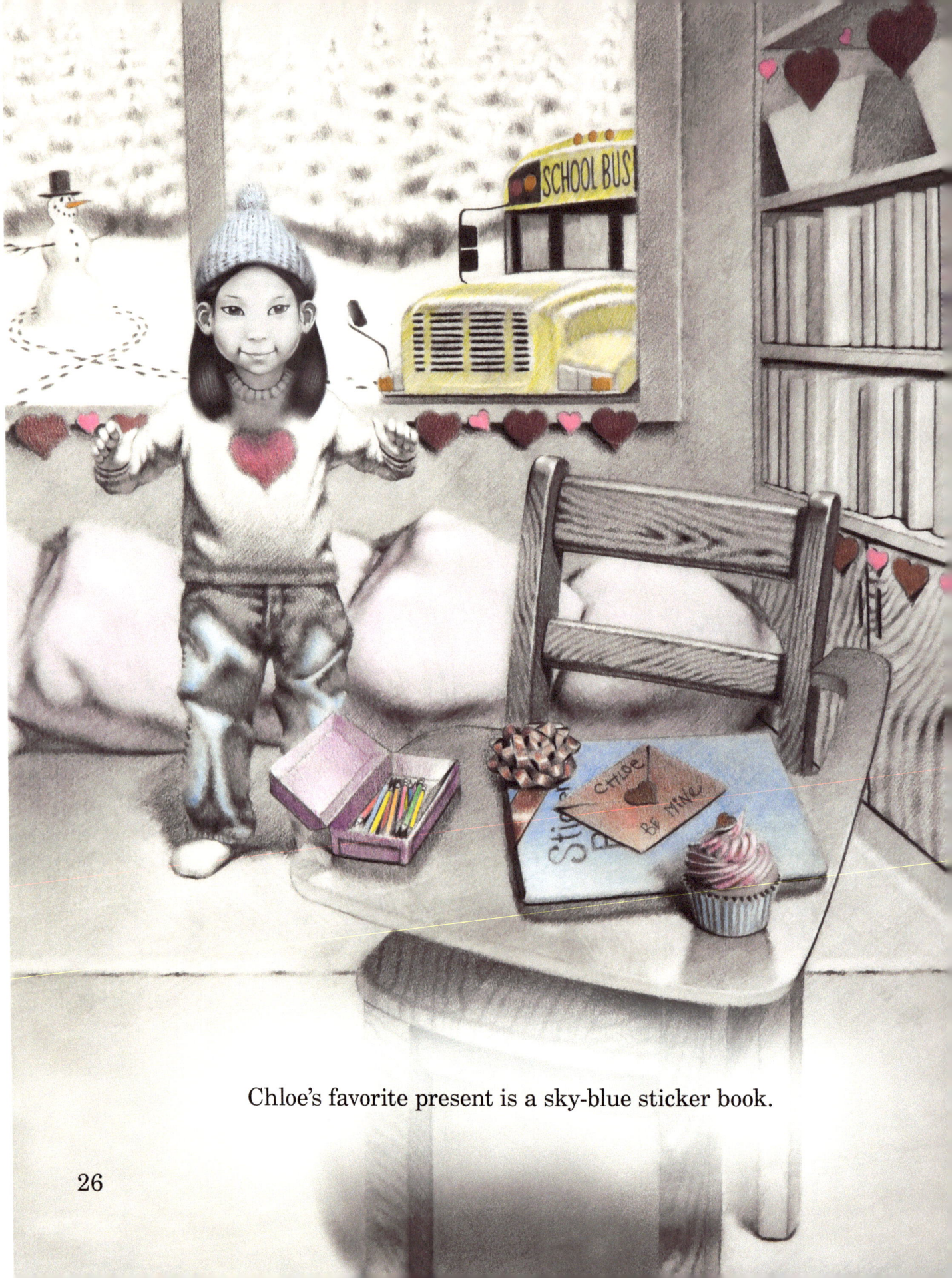

Chloe's favorite present is a sky-blue sticker book.

With sparkly stars and smelly fruit,

It's really worth a look!

When pages bloom like flowers,

In a garden filled with sun,

She dances with her sticker book;

The fun is never done!

"I love you, favorite present;

You fill my heart with glee!

My life got so much better,

The day you came to me."

Love

 glee

Day me

Stanley's favorite present is a boat with bright white sails.

When breezes kiss his sailboat, it's the gift that never fails.

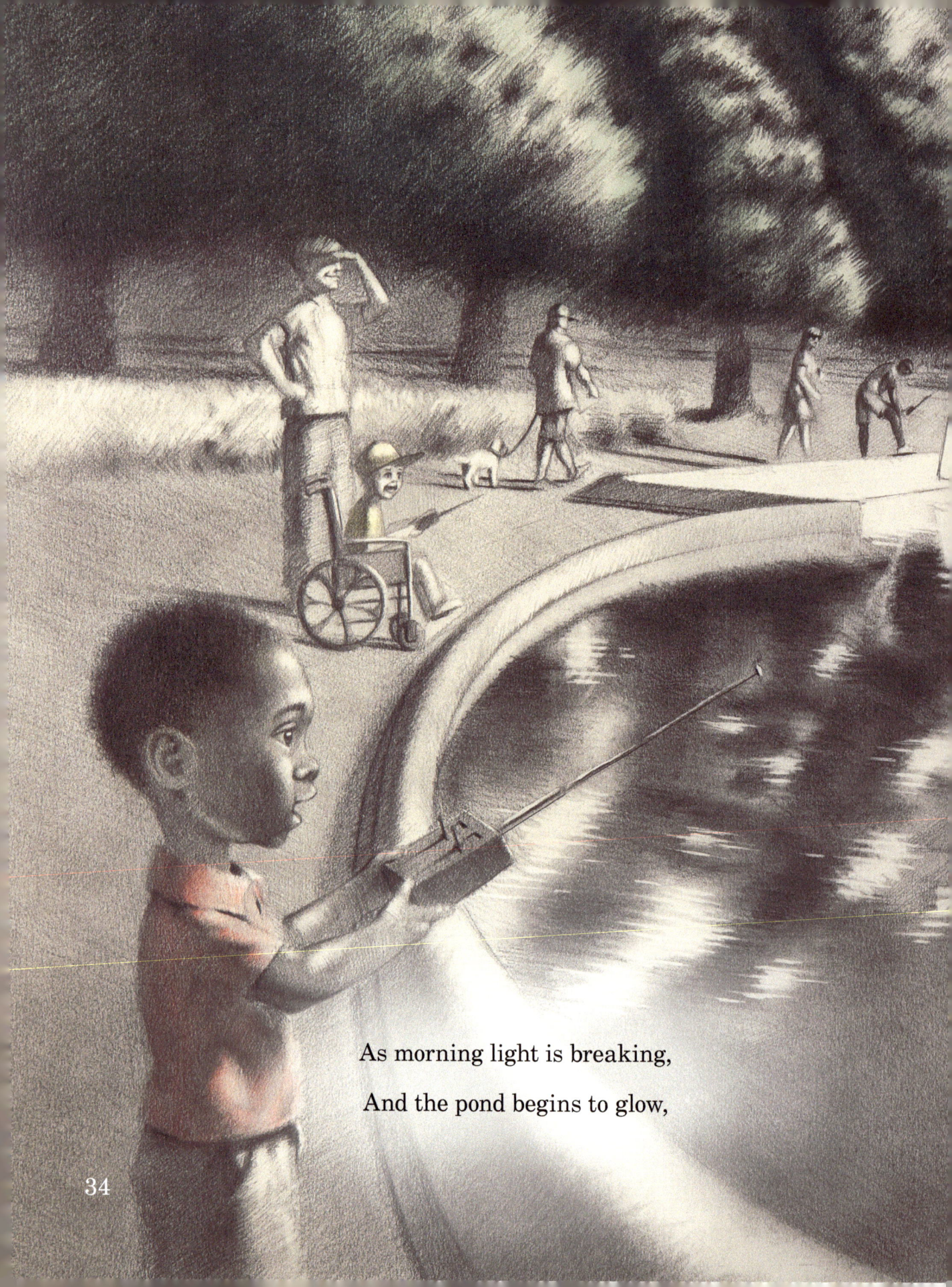

As morning light is breaking,

And the pond begins to glow,

He races toward the water,

And he smiles when breezes blow.

"I love you, favorite present;

You fill my heart with glee!

My life got so much better,

The day you came to me."

There's someone right beside you

With a favorite present too.

"If you want to know my secret,

I can share some clues with you."

"My present is quite different

From the ones that came before;

This gift is a real person

With a smile that I adore."

"As wonderful as music, warm as sunshine, strong as trees,

And sweet like golden honey from the flying honeybees."

"Like dolphins leaping from the waves,

Atop a turquoise ocean,

My favorite present is the gift

That sets my heart in motion."

"Like eagles soaring in the skies,

When mountain winds are blowing,

My favorite present is the gift

That's wild and free and growing!"

"Can I share my favorite present?

The gift that I look to?"

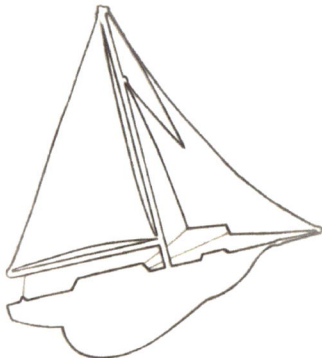

"Well, my darling little one,

My favorite present's…"

45

"You!"

attach photo here
2.5" x 3.75"

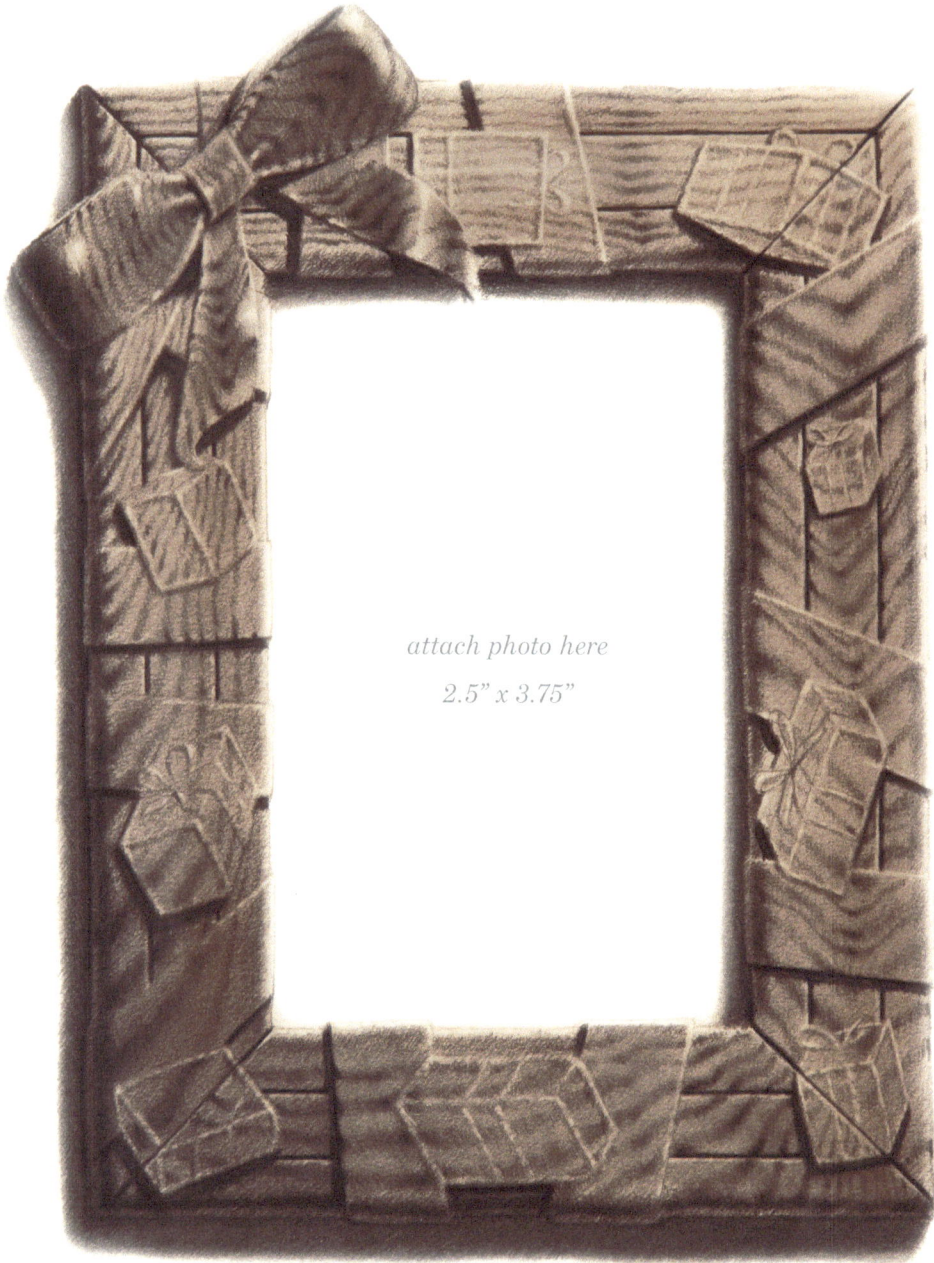

"When I watch you learn and laugh, it brightens up my day!

I feel so proud of who you are in every single way."

"And if one day there's distance

Between your hand and mine,

When our hands join once again,

My heart and soul will shine."

"I love you, favorite present;

You fill my heart with glee!

My life got so much better,

The day you came to me."

48

There is no

The End

To our story,

As our story will continue forever...